Parachute Silk

To ~~████~~

Love

Denise Bennett

Denise
18.9.15.

Oversteps Books

First published in 2015 by   Oversteps Books Ltd
6 Halwell House
South Pool
Nr Kingsbridge
Devon
TQ7 2RX
UK

www.overstepsbooks.com

Copyright © 2015 Denise Bennett
ISBN 978-1-906856-55-7

Printed in Great Britain by imprint digital, Devon

For my mother, Ada Amelia Bailey
14th March 1912–10th July 2014

Acknowledgements:

Some of these poems have appeared in the following magazines and anthologies: Acumen, Ariadne's Thread, Hardy Society Journal, Heart Shoots – Indigo Dreams Anthology, Interpreter's House, Obsessed With Pipework, Octopus Templar Poetry Anthology, Poetry and All That Jazz – Chichester Festivities Anthology, Poetry Nottingham, Poetry Society Newsletter, Quaker Voices, Rialto, Running Before The Wind – Grey Hen Anthology, Her Wings of Glass – Second Light Anthology, South, Weyfarers.

The Foundling Hospital was awarded 1st Prize in Hastings Poetry Competition 2012
Parachute Silk was awarded 1st Prize in Havant Literary Festival 2103
The Ring was runner up for the Hamish Canham Prize 2014

Grateful thanks to thanks to the artist Judes Crow, whose work inspired the sequence of poems about the sinking of the Royal George; and to Heather Johnson of the National Museum of the Royal Navy for her invaluable help in tracing the letter from William Trimmer. Special thanks to Maggie Sawkins for her guidance in assembling the collection, and to my husband Tom for his assistance in preparing the manuscript and for the cover picture.

Contents

The Foundling Hospital

Established in 1739 and opened by Thomas Coram 1741

Desperate mothers left their babies here
with scraps of fabric as identity tags
pinned to the admission slip;
one portion retained
to reclaim them later.

Silk, satin, cotton, these sad rags,
torn textiles a testament of love.
Linen, lawn, flannel,
where women tacked initials,
dates of birth in shaky stitches.

Some snipped bits of cloth
printed with buds, birds, butterflies, acorns,
to symbolise, a new life opening,
a child flying free, fruitful times to come ...
Waiting for the ballot,

white ball in,
black ball out,

mothers queued with their infants;
young lives hanging by threads,
calico, gingham muslin,
to claim a place.
Cambric, chintz, handmade lace;

babies swatched at birth.
Camblet, fustian, cherryderry,
names of material long gone,
cut from their own clothes,
recorded in hefty ledgers.

On leaving her son, one mother
cut his shirt clean in half,
wanted no mistake when retrieving him.
Another deposited one tiny sleeve.
Each left, clutching her grief.

Redemption

Foundling Hospital London 1767

It was just a bit of rag
a scrap of fabric, all she had
to remember him by

that cold February day
when Sarah Bender left her baby
Charles at the hospital;

a snip of patchwork ribbon
worked with a red running stitch,
which she'd split in two,

tearing the crumpled cloth,
the embroidered heart.
One half she kept

the other initialled piece
pinned to the admission slip
until she could redeem him.

They changed his name
to Benjamin Twirl;
wet-nursed and fattened

with country air, in time
he returned to school
in city grime, until

after eight years Sarah
came to claim him, matching
her tattered heart with his.

The Watch
Foundling Hospital First Intake 25th March 1741

I don't know who cried
the most that first day,
those who had their babies taken in
or those they turned away.

After they closed the doors at twelve
a knot of weeping women
were ordered to clear the street.
There was no scene more touching
as the two I witnessed.
One was clutching a small
bundle of squirming rags, sobbing
Oh my baby, my baby,
I can't feed him, I can't keep him,
the other twisting a pink ribbon
in her hands, her waxed face
drained of tears, wailing,
'Lily, oh my Lily.' Her empty arms
cradling her memory.

I don't know who
cried the most that first day,
those who had their babies taken in
or those they turned away.

Hearsay

I was the sickly twin
she named Emma, left
at The Foundling Hospital
with topknot of silk ribbons
pinned to my gown,
E.H. worked in gold.

No semaphore message
was sent to Nelson
anchored at Torbay,
announcing safe delivery,
only a secret letter telling
the birth of Horatia.

But I was a child
of the dancing mother,
the sailor father – the ailing sister
succoured by strangers
followed by historians
until the trail went cold.

I wonder, before she left
me, did she cuddle
me close in that space
between shoulder and chin,
the space that only
a mother knows?

What happened

after the hanging
when the black flag fluttered,
when Angel and Liza joined hands
and went on?

Tell me they went
to beg her body,
and held her in their arms,
stroked her hair
kissed her, as only a husband
and sister will do.

Tell me they bathed
the rope marks on her neck,
wrapped her in clean linen,
bore her home in a coffin to Marlott
where the villagers quietly came
to welcome her.

Tell me they buried her
alongside her child;
a proper funeral,
with hymns, prayers – the Parson there –
no skulking around
at the dead of night.

Tell me they didn't have
to hack back the nettles
in that sad spot where
the suicides and the drunkards go –
that her mother had kept
her grandson's grave tidy.

Tell me they laid flowers
and erected a headstone
which said:
In loving memory of Tess
and her dear son Sorrow.
Tell me, tell me
this is what happened.

Kilmainham Gaol Dublin

For Alice Kelly aged eight

Children as young as seven,
arrested for stealing bread
or turnips, were sent here
to tread the slabs, which covered
the bones of those who'd died
in cramped stinking cells;

children like Alice Kelly
who stole a coat to keep warm
were paraded in the exercise yard
round and round and round,
shunted like livestock;

children, thin as the wind
who tramped in rings, heads bowed,
eyes down on the heels
of the one in front,
knowing that looking skyward
would mean a beating.

Get your 'ead down.
You thieving scum,
you ain't fit to look at 'eaven.

Today, outside the gates
a child plays a penny whistle –
tourists throw coins.

Daughter

Someone wanted to adopt you
but you were mine.

Someone wanted to swathe you in a fine shawl
but you were mine.

Someone wanted to dress you in silk,
rock you in a wicker crib,

raise you as their own child
but you were mine.

And I clothed you in hand-me-downs,
wrapt you in a blanket,

laid you in a drawer, and kept you,
because you were mine.

Croup

He came on a Sunday afternoon,
kicking and screaming.
His father was the first to hold him
our son with the lusty lungs.
The first year was fine
then he got sick.

All night
he barked like a seal.
We filled the room with steam
to ease his breathing.
The doctor came.

In hospital
his throat closed.
A panic button summoned
a team in green coats to save him.
I ran after them.
We raced down a white corridor;
they shut the theatre doors in my face.

Alone in the hospital chapel
I ask God for the words I need
to tell Emily her brother is dead.
I cry a lot,
remember today is his 1st birthday.
21st March, the first day of spring.

Back in the ward.
He's on the critical list.
Intubated croup they say.
His throat is mute.
They have by-passed his voice box.
Even though he screams
I cannot hear him.
It's like a TV with the sound turned down.

A priest comes to baptise the baby
in the next cubicle.
Her name is Joanne.

I cannot hold him,
his hands are tied to
the sides of the cot
to stop him pulling his tubes.
We live like lepers in a glass box.
I sleep beside him for a week
willing him to live.

The eighth day. He's safe
they say he'll grow up to be strong;
he can breathe on his own,
the ventilator has gone.
I gather him into my arms.

Early April we take him home.
The world is full of daffodils,
the yellowness hurts my eyes.
Today Emily gets her boy-doll back,
wants to play with him.

We have a belated birthday party.
I bake a chocolate cake,
we sing, light the brightest candle
we can find.
He claps his hands and laughs,
and we cry.

Buried Language

She found the words
buried in a strong box
at the bottom of the wardrobe.

Complainant instead of mother.
Defendant instead of father.
Female bastard child instead of daughter.

A family jostling in heavy black type
along the folds of an old legal document.
*Seventeen shillings and sixpence a week
until sixteen – unless **it** dies.*

Unspeakable words,
her mother has locked in her throat
all those years ago.

Proposal

Standing at the sink
washing up, my son lets slip
his good news

as gently
as the bone-china plates
he is balancing on the drainer.

Last night, I proposed to Stuart
he says.
Love spills from his mouth

and I pick up his words
so casually dropped,
raise them, like a beacon.

Sixty Children Lost

Inspired by an exhibition of sixty doll-size clay heads by the artist, Judes Crow, in Portsmouth Museum commemorating the loss of sixty children on board the Royal George which sank in 1782.

Plum, peach, apple pie
how many years before I die?
One, two, three four ...

I hear happy children playing,
chanting skipping rhymes. Happy times.

Jump skip, jump rope, jump ship.

I find a plastic doll's head
washed ashore at Ryde;
reminder of sixty children lost
when the Royal George capsized.

It was Families' Day, women
and children aboard
when the captain ordered the ship
to be heeled to fix the water cock,
the time when barrels of rum,
livestock and rations were taken on.
She listed too far and gravity
took her portside down.

Some ran up the ratlines
to save their skin as she floundered,
few could swim, nine hundred drowned.
If I turn a rope I can say their names –

Mary, Sally, Robert, John
please will the next one follow on

Afterwards, fishermen feared
their catch: dismembered bodies,
half eaten heads of children in their nets.

Boatmen hauled the dead,
buried scores in shrouds of sand
along Ryde shore to sleep
to the sound of the waves.

Plum, peach, apple pie
how many years before I die?
One, two, three four ... jump skip, jump rope, jump ship.

I search the cliffs for clay;
at Yaverland, find rich brown
at Brook soft yellow, Luccombe
yields a leather-hard grey. I soak
the clay in water, begin to shape,
the children will live again,
I hear them say

and the ship came up and she wasn't sunk
and we all went home
and turned the rope.

Plum, peach, apple pie
how many years before I die?
One, two three four ... jump skip, jump rope, jump ship.

Swimming with a sheep

The Royal George capsized in 1782 in the Solent – 900 died including
60 children – one small boy was saved by clinging to the back of a sheep.

as the ship listed
      we ran up the ratlins

my sister fell I saw her drown
      the ladder burnt my hands

it was harder than the rope
      we skipped with in the yard

then I slipped and fell
      hit the water and I saw

a sheep swimming in the sea
      I'd seen her loaded into the hold

she'd have been the captain's dinner
      my Dad told me but she was alive

a lad in a sailor suit climbed
      on her back and she swam

and a man in a wherry boat
      hauled him in and saved him

and he saved the sheep too
      but I drowned and sleep now

in the sands at Ryde no tide to
      take me home to the yard

where I turned the rope

each, peach, apple pie
how many years
before I die
one, two,
three four ...

The Carpenter

In 1782 the Royal George sank in the Solent while she was being heeled over for repairs. HMS Victory picked up many survivors.

... and they carried his body
down to *Victory's* belly,
laid him on the hearth
before the galley fire.

Women tried to revive him,
chafe his hands to warmth,
put brandy to his lips.
The man they cradled

had tried to right the ship,
twice cried a warning
to the watch and been ignored
before the waters came.

Dismissed, he drowned as
the *Royal George* went down;
floating with hen-coops
hammocks and splintered masts.

No plaque marks where he lay;
No one speaks his name.

Wedding Garland

Based on an extract from a letter of an officer of the fleet.

... and they laid them down
on the beach, in the ale houses
those they'd ferried home:

women, children, pressed men
who had gathered
under a Wedding Garland,

on the ship;
an evergreen sphere decked
with white satin streamers,

the signal for wives
and sweethearts to sing and dance
and say goodbye.

They laid them down in alehouses
about the Point,
and on the stones to die.

Jack Lamb

Jack Lamb rode
the glittering skirt of sea
on the back of a sheep,
his tiny fists clutching
the wool so tightly
we had to cut away the fleece
to free him –

the half-drowned waif,
who when the wherry's keel
grated on the shingle
at Sally Port,
called for his Mother and Father
as we hauled in.

Thursday Last

Based on William Trimmer's letter – eye witness to the sinking of
the Royal George 1782.

Dear Mama

Remember me to Mr Roberts,
let me know how he does.
Thank Betsy for minding my tools,
tell her I hope she's better soon.
Went ashore, received some money
to sort out my clothes as befits
a Midshipman. Much time is taken up
reading scriptures and psalms.
I suppose you have heard of
the shocking accident which happened
Thursday last of the Royal George –
she being deep-heeled for repairs,
the Lieutenant paying no heed
to water coming into her ports, she overset
and sank. There were dead men
and women floating in hammocks, hats,
pigs floating on pieces of spare masts,
fowls and geese, hen-coops, chests;
a blue coat belonging to Admiral Kempenfeldt
sticking up against the deck.
No less than nine hundred souls lost.

Tinkers, hawkers, old salts, peddlers,
prostitutes, signalmen, powder monkeys,
plumbers, wives, women and sixty children
all pitched into the tarry sea and drowned,
save one orphan lad they named Jack Lamb
who clung to a sheep as it swam.

Give my love to Papa Grandpapa,
aunts and uncles. I am, Mama, your affectionate son

William Trimmer

No Names

And they brought us home in a fishing net,
me and the others, all meshed together,
a shoal of children who drowned in the wreck.

The trawlermen who caught us, won't forget
that morning in fair September weather
when they brought us home in a fishing net.

No names were recorded in a gazette:
Billy, baby John, light as a feather
the shoal of children who drowned in the wreck,

sons and daughters without an epithet
who stumbled and fell, ran hell for leather.
And they brought us home in a fishing net,

children who once laughed, danced and sang who met
with death, those they would willingly tether.
The shoal of children who drowned in the wreck

who now lie in a mass grave. People regret
that they can't call us, Edward or Heather.
And they brought us home in a fishing net
a shoal of children who drowned in the wreck.

Resurrection

Here is the stump of stone
with weathered ship and anchor;
words worn away –

underneath, the bones of those
who died. And I dream
of a honey-coloured sun,

a Van Gogh blue sky,
the time when the sod will rise,
children come shouldering

through dark earth
to skip and sing, shaking
the crumbs of soil from

their limbs: *Mary, Sally,*
Robert John, please
will the next one follow on.

The Cobb

Lyme Regis

That wild September night
walking on the Cobb at Lyme
we saw the boiling black sea
like dirty laundry water
dashing against the Portland stone,
felt the wuthering wind whipping our hair,
our bodies like flagpoles, clothes blowing.
We saw the scum ribbons of foam;
and granny's teeth, those jagged steps
where Jane Austen's heroine fell –
tasted the salt spray which stung our eyes
as we clung to each other.

Next day retracing our steps,
to the bay, we passed the cottage
where Captain Benwick lived,
found the harbour a topazine pool of blue,
white frilled waves, delicate as the lace
on Louisa Musgrove's dress.

Hovercraft Accident

Ryde – Southsea 1972

Head down, a woman
shuffles along the shore,
pays no attention to the waves,
her feet pecking at the debris.
She wipes her tears
bends to gather a handful of shells,
enough for a necklace –

remembering her child
eager for the sea, a day trip,
with her uncle, a birthday treat;
recalls the wash of the ferry,
the upturned hovercraft caught
in a wall of white water –
the breaking news.

Great Storm

16th October 1987

That night I was not
soft as spindrift,
a sea-salt zephyr breeze
but a hurly-burley
razzamatazzy, surly
sing-song wind,
a howling ghoul,
gusting, blustering
a whirling Dervish
spinning slates,
hitting windows,
breaking glass
blowing a hooley,
a hullabaloo,
ripping off roof tops.
That night I lashed
the back of Shanklin Pier,
broke it into three pieces,
spewed it into the sea.
I damaged fencing which
unleashed a rampage
of wild boars,
flipped planes, easy as Airfix,
reduced beach huts,
caravans to tinder.
I slew a man
sleeping rough in London,
killed firemen, sailors,
blanked out the capital
blocked roads with debris,
ran harum-scarum,
tore through the woods.
This was my greatest sprint
since 1703. That night
I felled 15 million trees.

Inspection

After Inspection *by Wilfred Owen*

He found me *dirty* on parade
with blood-stained battledress.
It's my own blood sir, I said.
The sergeant took my name.

Out, damned spot!
I cried, as I rubbed the cloth,
the day the Captain came
and found me confined to camp –
doing penance for my cheek.

The Sergeant sent me here Sir
to mend my ways, to wash away
my sin. Like Lady Macbeth,
I say, *Out, damned spot*!

But the shirt will not clean.
In my head I see the blood
of friends spilling, drop
by drop, bright, scarlet seeds
of comrades dying.

It's a game, a whitewash afoot –
all cut and dried. A plot
to speed young men to their death;
we're all washing out our dirty linen.

And what will God say Sir
when the Generals
have bled the troops dry;
when he inspects the men
and you have hung us out to die?

No Reply

Death of Edward Thomas 9th April 1917

That day I was
embroidering a wild duck on a postcard
as a present for my Daddy;

a heap of wools at my side,
yellow, green, brown all to be stitched
into drake feathers, a mallard in flight,

a bird writing in the sky,
sending a message to France –
Come home. Come home. Its lonely cry.

It was a bright, April day,
the hedgerow bursting with white violets;
when I saw the telegram boy lean his

red bike against the gate.
I waited with *chilled heart and dry mouth*
as mother read the words

Then croaked out – *No reply.*

Welcome

After First Time In *by Ivor Gurney 1890–1937*

You should have heard
those four Welsh lads from the valleys
singing in the trenches:
David of the White Rock, the *Slumber song*.
All pals together.

You should have seen them
welcome me with food, candles,
kindness; sharing parcels from home.
Me trembling at the newness of it all
listening to the colony of pit boys
in sandbag ditches, their voices
breaking my heart; novice colliers
who'd swapped coal dust for mud.

That first evening, I held their faces
lit by the glow of soft light,
watched them mouth Welsh lullabies
under the sound of the guns;
words learnt in their cradles.

Sleep my child and peace attend thee
All through the night.
Guardian angels God will send thee,
All through the night.

Nothing could blot out
my beautiful entry to that sacred trench,
nor take away that moment of hope.

Sinking of The Royal Oak

i.m. the 125 boy seamen who perished on the Royal Oak *14th October 1939*

Don't worry mum there's nothing doing
we're sailing to Scapa Flow,
we'll be tucked away. I'm safer than you.

Discipline was tough.
Cuts from the cane and jankers
for those caught with a whiff
of baccy on their breath –
those boy sailors, some underage,
Nelson's blind eye turned.

Look on the bright side.
I'm nearly sure I'll get leave for Christmas.
You wouldn't think there was a war on.
It's so quiet.

They trained in stone frigates
as messengers, telegraphers, signalmen.
One hundred and twenty five died
the night the ship was hit
including a band boy, only fifteen.

Give baby Beverley a kiss from me.
And tell her that her big brother Stan will
soon be back to swing her up high, high to the sky.
I do miss her ...

I could weep when I think
of all those lads who drowned
their lungs filling with liquid tar,
no more than two bob and a tanner
in their pockets, the only pay
they were allowed to keep...

I'm well and happy. Look after yourself.
Tell Alf to put the kettle on and shift that lazy dog
Barnaby away from the fire. I'll soon be home.

Your loving son
Stan

The Nightingales and the Lancaster Bombers

Desert Island Discs chosen by Vikram Seth 27th January 2012

This was his favourite disc,
because, he said
It represents joy and pain.

On his desert island
he would listen again
to the sound of nightingales

and the Lancaster Bombers
recorded on a summer evening in 1942;
hear them spilling

their silvery song
in a Surrey spinney filling
the air with hope,

absorb the trill of these shy,
rufus-brown birds
almost drowned by the sound

of one hundred and ninety seven
planes soaring in the sky,
engines roaring to war.

Mr Smith

did his bit for victory,
turned his flower garden
into a vegetable patch;

planted beans, peas, and greens
but in between
he sowed a row of gladioli;

a slender chorus line
of spiky, bright flowers
which kept him sane he said

especially on dark nights
down in the Anderson, listening
to the *dog fights*.

Under the bomber's moon
he imagined his flowers
dancing in their scarlet

and apricot frocks
amongst the unfurling fans
of the cabbages.

Portsmouth Women in War

Let's blow a bugle for city women,
those left at home who scrimped for coal
to stoke the fires they kept burning, who queued
in rain for scrag end meat, learning
to make meals with *Marguerite Patten*,
becoming dab hands with powdered egg.
Those who curried favour with spivs
for tins of cling peaches and spam;
who pencilled stocking seams
on gravy-browned legs, a bit of glam
for the Saturday hop, who stood in lines
whenever a consignment of silk stockings
came to McIlroys, the department shop.

No one has written these names in gold
nor raised a statue to their glory,
or told how it was to give birth in an air-raid,
how they shushed crying children in damp
Andersons, counselling the bereaved,
the bombed out, with oceans of hot, sweet, tea.
No one speaks about Mrs Wheatley
who lost her baby daughter in the blitz,
whose name they tucked away in
the dusty pages of a council list; and so
for Nora, Sylvia, Betty, Maureen,
Edna and Iris, always praying for the beacon
of an orange to bring them through – I salute you.

Parachute Silk

This quiet cloth, colour
of a dove's egg, designed as canopies
for soft landings

cut down, could turn
any bride into
a gardenia or edelweiss.

Esther had chased hers
across fields with a pitchfork
when a German airman landed.

Ruth had received hers
from her fiancé who'd used it
as a pillow, when injured;

Eva's boss had simply opened
a cupboard and found one
still with the ropes intact,

sensuous as spindrift.
Snipped and pinned, slipped over waist
and hips, this soft silk would grace

wartime weddings. The lives
of those men cut down, living on
in tuck and pleat and fold.

Without You

In the brief blue flame of dusk
flowers exhale their breath
night begins to cool.

       I close the curtains
       set the table with one plate,
       knife, fork, spoon.

Tomorrow under a gash
of white sky, I will listen
again for the larks

       we used to hear,
       watch them criss-crossing the air
       stitching the torn canopy.

Paper Chains

They kept us quiet for hours
those sixpenny sheaves
thin, coloured slips; pink

yellow, green and blue,
strips we would lick and stick
like joining up the relatives

linking Devon cousins and Uncles
with Great Aunts who went to America
at the time of the *Titanic;*

those known only by faded photos,
spidery hands on flimsy air-mails
and Christmas cards; every chain

a name; unbroken family ties
we hung from the walls, each one
fixed with the kissy-spit of love.

James Squire
1843 – 1929

Her Grandfather used to farm this way
driving his doe-eyed herd
through rime frost and Queen Anne's lace
frothing in the Devon lane,
the scent of cows in his hair.

He knew the miracle of butter
the gift of turning the churn,
watching his wife coax the yellow
grains of fat to gold. In spring
he went looking for oxlips
in glimmering light. In winter
he gathered holly for the hearth.

The parish register records
the rhythm of his life,
his marriage, the baptism
and burial of four of his thirteen children –
the burial of his wife.

Country Girl

she came from
cart-ruts, fox-prints, rabbit tracks
set in red Devon earth,

from corn sheaves
sewn from seed-fiddle and plough,
poppies among the wheat crops;

from squabble and squawk
with brothers at the pump, gulping down
pure blue water,

from the scum of lace
on a Sunday dress, coolness of choir stalls
a soprano singing out her faith –

bed-ridden now, displaced by cityscape
she still listens for the cows
lowing in the lane

Handleys

She used to come here before the war
when there were linen tablecloths,
silver service, when white-capped waitresses
in black, flew around the floor.

Each Friday she escorted her mistress
three o'clock, on the dot,
to sip a cup of Earl Grey whilst listening
to the Hungarian orchestra play.

Sometimes she imagined herself
letting down her long red hair
stamping in a scarlet-swirl skirt
to make the tea cups rattle;

mostly though, she sat demure,
with Mrs Raphael on a table that faced the sea,
observed the ritual of pastry forks,
the tremble of the gypsy fiddle,

watched as women with tiny hats
clamped to Marcel waves, dispensed
with their lace gloves, ordered tea-cakes
or scones in the flap of a napkin

while she sat in her neat, navy suit,
a grass widow, hugging a bundle
of blue-ribboned letters to her heart,
clocking up the days to his home-coming.

Each week she stashed her dreams
in the bank, sometimes there was extra pay
when Madam fancied Mantovani on a Wednesday.
Every note building her bungalow.

Clovelly

The tide of war began
to turn in forty four,

and she wanted things
back the way they were.

A lick of paint
on the name plate – *Clovelly,*

the odd-job man
to mend the broken fence,

fix the leaky tap,
tack down the worn stair carpet;

Mr Johns, the sweep,
to bristle the chimney clean –

all made ready.
These things she did – and there was

a fire blazing in the grate,
a stew simmering on the stove,

and their baby son was asleep
in his crib when

the telegram boy
leaned his bike against the gate.

Lazarus Event

For Ada aged 97

When they took away
her drugs, food and water,
told me she would die,
I watched her skin
turn marble white,
sat quietly praying by her bed.

Outside, the Easter trees
rocked in their grief.
On the third day she woke up
and asked for tea.

Window

For Ada aged 99

What's it like out? she asks.
She has no weather now
they have moved her chair from the window;

to a safe, dry, sterile place.
She feels no sun or air on her face,
hears no rattle of rain,

no wind teases her hair.
Words like blazing, teaming,
drizzle, flurry, breezy

have rusted on her tongue.
She remembers her trust
of blue sky, laundry days.

Outside the golden wheels
of sunflowers turn, she tells
of a time when she took tea

to her uncles on the farm,
harvesting under sweltering heat;
speaks of her favourite season,

kicking up the fallen leaves.
I catch her drift, wish for the gift
of a window to sustain her.

My Mother's Shoes

For Ada aged 100

At five my mother wore loose boots
her brothers had worn, stuffed with rags
or torn paper; two sizes too big,
filled with the history of their lives.
Each day she skidded over fields,
to the village school.

In mid-life she had a fetish
for sexy black stilettos,
tap-clacking on lino or polished floors
of dance halls, her feet taut as arrows.
Each night she teetered on spindle heels,
grew to five foot three.

In old age she bought comfort shoes
from charity shops:
satin pumps, *worn once for a wedding*,
red lace-ups, low heeled suede slip-ons.
Each day she trudged round the town
wearing down the weight of other lives.

At ninety eight, when she craved
something pretty,
I got her soft leather, silver slippers.
For one brief moment, I was Dandini,
she was Cinderella.
They nestle *unworn,* in her wardrobe.

She rarely gets out of bed now

Grandma's 100th Birthday

She came at a quiet moment
a few days after you were born
held your leaf-curled hand as you slept.

I shall never see him grow up,
he's come late in my life, she said.
Thirty years on you come to her

in a quiet moment. She sleeps,
wakes as you take her leaf-curled hand
to slip a bracelet on her wrist;

a grandson's special birthday gift,
bangle of red, green and white beads,
which she will fiddle with and love.

No camera could capture this touch;
the time when her thin, puckered skin,
brushed against your bright wedding ring.

The Ring

For Ada aged 101

We found it slipped
between the sheets, she said

as she handed me my
mother's engagement ring.

It had never left her finger
since her sailor beau had proposed

seventy seven years ago,
kissing her tide of red hair –

and I took the delicate band,
whittled thin with seventy years

of widowhood, and carried her
grief out into the rain.

Handbag

When she dies
I will fill her handbag with:
family photos, love letters,
a Max Factor Compact,
a bottle of *Coty L'Aimant*,
a slick red lip-stick – Passion Fire,
a small leather purse, full of coins,
and a bunch of house-keys –
all the things they took from her.

It was *untidy, in the way*, they said.
They couldn't deal with her whimpering
whenever she lost it.
Didn't want to understand
her whole world was weighted there.

In her last years she made
a nest of treasures in a tissue box.
A pink tail-comb, a lip-salve,
glasses, a Remembrance Day poppy
and a tiny bible which we bought her.

In the hall
they have certificates
about dignity, caring for the elderly,
gold stars for hygiene,
notes on nutrition,
the treatment of bed sores and wounds
and how to handle the residents – safely.
The day they took her life
is not written down.

Touching

For Ada aged 101

I bring her rose perfume
made by monks on Caldey Island;

each Friday and Sunday
consecrate her body,

anoint her temples and neck,
dab her pulse points.

I am relearning the gift of touch,
flesh on flesh.

She knows me now
by the scent that I carry

and yesterday she took my hand,
and kissed my fingers

the way she did
on the day that I was born.

The Miracle

Throughout the hot summer
the fungus grew on her head
like a death-cap mushroom.
There was no cure,
only a treatment of antiseptic and honey,
and a cardboard dome.

They had mentioned radiation,
just one shot but it was risky,
she was too old to move.
I prayed for a miracle
and a few days later
a fly laid eggs in her open wound.

Under the festering dressing
the maggots grubbed up a banquet;
polished off her rotting flesh,
leaving her skin pink and clean.
*Done more good than gamma rays
ever could* the shocked staff said.

I was told she screamed
with pain and itching;
frenzied hands had clawed her head –
and those who found her
and the fat maggots writhing in the bed
couldn't eat their lunch, they said.

Some Days

Monday

Barrie's dead, she says.
Don't be silly, I say. He signed the visitors'
book yesterday, so he can't be.
Have a dolly mixture, I say. She likes them.
That Hazel Ford keeps taking my clothes.
Hazel lives in Shoreham, I say.
She hasn't seen you for forty years.
Why have they put me in black gloves?
She lifts her arms. I pretend to take off
the long, black evening gloves.
Where did they get these? I ask.
My hands brush hers. She pulls away.
She was never one for touching.

Tuesday

Look at my face, she says.
My skin is all dry. I try not to look
at the crater on her nose where a large
cancer has come and gone,
or the white, domed dressing which hides
another cancer, big as a death-cap mushroom.
They measure it each month, take photos.
I take out the Max Factor compact,
the sterile puff, pretend to powder her face.
She knows it's make-believe,
there's no scent, only the smell of dead flesh.

Wednesday

Where's my shoes? she asks.
The silver ones you got me?
You can't wear your shoes, you're in bed, I say.
No I'm not, I'm sitting in a chair. I'm not
in bed. She's quite adamant.

Would you like to hold them?
I'll fetch them, I say. I rummage in her cupboard
and take out the never worn, silver pumps
which I bought her four years ago
when she was Cinderella and I was Dandini.
I want to put them on, she says.
You're in bed, you don't need shoes,
you're in bed, I say. Her delicate, papery hands
skim the leather. She waves them away.
Where's my green fleece, the one you bought me?
I used to wear it in the wheelchair.
It's quite safe, I say. It's hanging up ...

Thursday

Give me some money. I want some money.
They've taken my bag. She holds out her hand.
You don't have money anymore, you don't
need it. I know how she longs to hold coins
in her hands – maybe she wants to tip the staff.
My eyes smart when I remember how they
took away her handbag. She holds her treasures now
in a tissue box. A lip-salve, a Remembrance Day poppy,
a pink tail-comb, a tiny bible ...
Give me some money, she pleads.
I try to distract her. Would you like a drink? I say.

Friday

Water. Water. I hold the beaker to her lips.
She snatches it, tries to guide it to the shrivelled
bud of her mouth. I try to help. She fights me,
pushes me away. Tries again to steer the spout.
Leave me alone! she screams.
Bitch! Bitch! You've only come here to cause trouble.
I'll just sit here I say. Who are you? she says.
I'm Denise, your daughter. I mop the wetness
from her neck. I'm just a black shadow.
How can I be her daughter?

Saturday

I stare at her filthy fingernails, the detritus
of food, faeces, dried blood where she has
been scratching her wound; her skinny fingers
where her rings hang slack. Already her engagement ring
has slipped between the sheets.
Do you want anything? I say.
She flinches when I touch her.
Why don't you go away and cut your tongue out.
I'll just get myself a cup of tea, I say.

Sunday

Her bed is shoved up against the wall;
the cot side is broken, she is asleep.
Her wound seeps and reeks; I ask the staff
to change and date the dressing –
we don't want maggots again.
I sit and read, keep watch.

Lines for a Bereaved Daughter

When the funeral director asks
what colour robe would you like your
mother to wear? Pink, blue, white, cream.
I go for blue – *Blue I say,*
she liked blue
she died in her blue cardigan.
It's just like picking a dress
from a catalogue. He jots it down.

Can I put her silver slippers in
her coffin?
Yes, he says.
I want to tell him that now
she will be Cinderella.
I want to explain but I can't find
the words – *and her handbag?*
She'll need her handbag
I want to say. They took it away
when she was in the home,
she grieved for years over that bag.
His kind eyes assent,
he's heard it all before.
I must make sure she is dressed,
has her silver slippers,
carries her comb, lipstick,
powder compact, scent, letters,
the picture postcards we wrote,
photos of her grandchildren –
her bible.

At the Chapel Of Rest

A kind young woman greets me
asks if my mother
has had an operation.
I say *she's had a nasty place*
on her head; I know about the dressing.

I open the door.
she is lying in her coffin
with a bandage around her head.
looks just like a little doll.
A doll in a box at Christmas.
She will be my wounded soldier dolly;
I'll put her into a Clarke's shoe box bed,
and nurse her better ...

The coffin is draped in blue velvet.
Her thin hands are crossed
onto her breast. I press a kiss
from my lips onto her tiny fingers.
I don't stay long.
I tuck her handbag in beside her,
slip her Cinderella shoes under the cover.
I want to fit them onto her feet
but the Dandini inside me has died.

Cure For Grief

i.m. of Ada Bailey 14.3.1912 – 10.7.2014

... you'll find a red van
which sells tea,
seats where you can sit
and watch the sea.

... and I found the red van,
and bought the tea,
and watched the waves shimmer
like a sky-blue dance dress,

remembering how
I'd nestled in her wardrobe
as a child, felt the prickle
of net skirts, the touch of taffeta;

how I'd stroked the black velvet bodices,
soft as her fox furs.
I could almost hear her
crooning Moonlight Serenade.

Oversteps Books Ltd

The Oversteps list includes books by the following poets:

David Grubb, Giles Goodland, Alex Smith, Will Daunt, Patricia Bishop, Christopher Cook, Jan Farquarson, Charles Hadfield, Mandy Pannett, Doris Hulme, James Cole, Helen Kitson, Bill Headdon, Avril Bruton, Marianne Larsen, Anne Lewis-Smith, Mary Maher, Genista Lewes, Miriam Darlington, Anne Born, Glen Phillips, Rebecca Gethin, W H Petty, Melanie Penycate, Andrew Nightingale, Caroline Carver, John Stuart, Rose Cook, Jenny Hope, Hilary Elfick, Jennie Osborne, Anne Stewart, Oz Hardwick, Angela Stoner, Terry Gifford, Michael Swan, Denise Bennett, Maggie Butt, Anthony Watts, Joan McGavin, Robert Stein, Graham High, Ross Cogan, Ann Kelley, A C Clarke, Diane Tang, Susan Taylor, R V Bailey, John Daniel, Alwyn Marriage, Simon Williams, Kathleen Kummer, Jean Atkin, Charles Bennett, Elisabeth Rowe, Marie Marshall, Ken Head, Robert Cole, Cora Greenhill, John Torrance, Michael Bayley, Christopher North, Simon Richey, Lynn Roberts, Sue Davies, Mark Totterdell, Ann Segrave, Helen Overell and Rose Flint.

For details of all these books, information about Oversteps and up-to-date news, please look at our website:

www.overstepsbooks.com